FOOTBALLERS EARN LESS THAN THEIR UNDERPANTS DO!

The fact or fiction behind

FOOTBALL

...utherland

WAYLAND

Published in paperback in 2014 by Wayland

Copyright © Wayland 2014

Wayland
338 Euston Road
London NW1 3BH

Wayland Australia
Level 17/207 Kent Street
Sydney, NSW 2000

Editor: Debbie Foy
Design: Rocket Design (East Anglia) Ltd
Illustration: Alan Irvine

British Library Cataloguing in Publication Data
Sutherland, Adam.
The fact or fiction behind football. -- (Truth or busted)
1. Soccer--Miscellanea--Juvenile literature.
2. Common fallacies--Juvenile literature.
I. Title II. Series
796.3'34'02-dc23

ISBN: 978 0 7502 8159 1

Printed in Great Britain, by CPI Group (UK) Ltd, Croydon, CR0 4YY
10 9 8 7 6 5 4 3 2 1

Wayland is a division of Hachette Children's Books,
an Hachette UK company
www.hachette.co.uk

All illustrations by Shutterstock, except 4, 16, 22, 32, 33, 38, 40, 44, 50, 76

EVERYTHING YOU KNOW ABOUT FOOTBALL COULD BE AS WRONG AS A THREE-LEGGED GOALKEEPER...

read on!

Read this bit first...!

Football, so they say, is a funny old game. Over hundreds of years, it has changed from large crowds of villagers kicking a pig's bladder around in the mud to a multi-billion pound sport watched and enjoyed around the world.

But along with the progress have come hundreds of half-truths and falsehoods. Did football really start a war, or stop one? Was the World Cup trophy really once stolen and found by a dog called Pickles? Did a fan actually sue his team for being rubbish?

The answers to these and dozens of other questions can be found inside **Truth or Busted**'s *Footballers Earn Less Than Their Underpants Do*. You'll also find our collection of bizarre quotes from the biggest names in the game, and a selection of truly amazing and unexpected footballing record-breakers. Once you've digested that lot, try the rib-tickling features on the daftest footballing injuries, funny players' nicknames, and some of the oddest goal celebrations known to the sporting world.

By the time you reach the final page of **Truth or Busted**'s *Footballers Earn Less Than Their Underpants Do*, we guarantee you'll be able to tell a footballing 'truth' from a footballing 'busted' on sight. Don't thank us — we do it because we love the game.

SO, FOOTBALL LOVERS, PREPARE TO BE AMAZED...

read on!

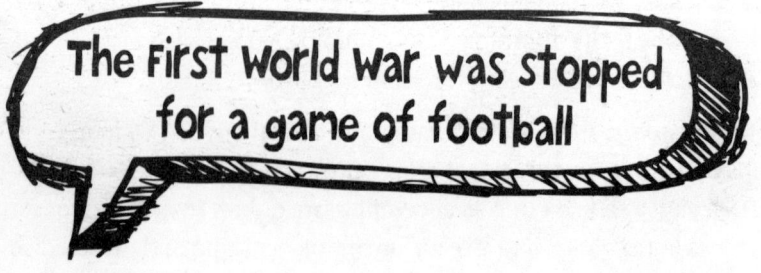

The First World War was stopped for a game of football

You can imagine it, can't you? 'Let's have a kick about, Fred. Watch out for landmines, though, or it'll be rather more than eleven a side.'

★ And the truth is...

Picture this: it's Christmas Day 1915, in the battlefields of Northern France. The shelling stops, and two groups of grubby, exhausted young men emerge from the trenches, putting aside their grievances temporarily to enjoy a festive game of football.

We don't know how or why it happened, but it's as true as Lionel Messi having short legs. We're not sure how much fun it was, though. One survivor, Bertie Felstead, remembers, 'It was about 50 a side. No one kept score.'

Interesting literary fact: one of Felstead's brothers in arms was the poet Robert Graves, who actually wrote about the event in a poem called *Christmas Interlude* (1929).

Verdict: _____ **TRUTH** _____

'WE LOST BECAUSE WE DIDN'T WIN'

The daftest football quotes collected

There's nothing funnier than a football commentator or player saying something daft. Luckily, it happens all the time! We have collected some of our favourites throughout this book. Feel free to laugh at their expense. We did!

'We lost because we didn't win'.

You can't argue with former Brazilian striker Ronaldo's logic

'Chile have three options - they could win or they could lose'.

Former England manager, Kevin Keegan, shows an impressive grasp of options. But not maths

A player was once murdered for scoring an own goal

We know players get a lot of stick from their team mates, and from fans, if they ever put the ball in their own net. But murder? Surely not...

⭐ And the truth is...

Colombia went into the 1994 World Cup in the USA as one of the favourites for the tournament. The betting back home was on them to do well. And then disaster struck. Needing a result against the USA, Colombian defender Andrés Escobar made a mess of an intended clearance, and put the ball into his own net. The team lost 2-1 and Colombia were out of the tournament.

Ten days later, Escobar was shot and killed outside a bar in his home city of Medellín by a man shouting 'Goal!' The killer, a local school teacher, was sentenced to 43 years in prison.

Verdict:  TRUTH

FOOTBALL RECORD BREAKERS

Rogério Ceni
....

The current Sao Paulo goalkeeper has
been his team's first choice in goal
for over 20 years. In this time he has
also proved himself more than capable
of finding the opposition's net as well
as protecting his own. Ceni has scored
a record-breaking 112 goals, most of
them from free kicks and penalties. In
one season he scored an incredible 21!

A fan sued his team for being rubbish

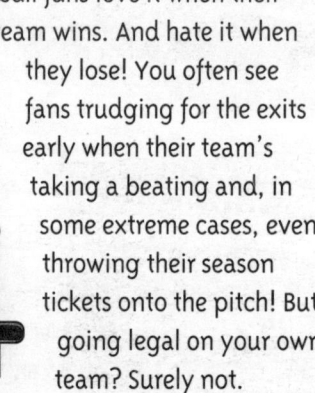

Football fans love it when their team wins. And hate it when they lose! You often see fans trudging for the exits early when their team's taking a beating and, in some extreme cases, even throwing their season tickets onto the pitch! But going legal on your own team? Surely not.

And the truth is...

Bob Montgomery, a fan of the English team Sheffield Wednesday, was so annoyed by his team's poor performance in the 1993 FA Cup Final against London-based club Arsenal that he sued the club under the Trades Description Act, claiming they had obtained money under false pretences — in other words, by calling themselves a professional football club! Bob's frustration was probably made worse by the fact that Sheffield Wednesday also lost to Arsenal in the League Cup Final a month earlier. Unfortunately, at least for many frustrated fans around the world, Bob lost the case.

Verdict: _____

'WE LOST BECAUSE WE DIDN'T WIN'

The daftest football quotes collected

'After 15 years, I'm an overnight success'.

Real Madrid manager José Mourinho

'I couldn't settle in Italy, it was like living in a foreign country'.

Allegedly the words of ex-Liverpool FC striker Ian Rush, who briefly played for Italian side Juventus — until he discovered they played abroad!

A national team once played against no opposition – and still drew!

Amazingly, this happened to the Scottish national team. But the important questions are: how do you end up playing a game of eleven players against none, and then, how can you not win?!?

And the truth is...

In 1996, Scotland were scheduled to play Estonia in a World Cup qualifier in the capital city Tallinn. The game was due to kick off at 6.45pm, but Scotland complained about the quality of the stadium's temporary floodlights (which were mounted on the backs of lorries) and FIFA moved the kick off forward to 3pm instead. Estonia officials protested, and the team refused to turn up for the game, which Scotland started and which was immediately abandoned. The chant from the Scottish travelling fans was, quite accurately, *'There's only one team in Tallinn'*. In case anyone asks you, the game was replayed in Monaco a month later and ended nil-nil!

Verdict: ___(mostly)___ TRUTH

'WE LOST BECAUSE WE DIDN'T WIN'

The daftest football quotes collected

'We must have had **99%** of the game. It was the other **3%** that cost us the match'.

Former Dutch international midfielder Ruud Gullit shows that his football was far better than his adding up

'Our major problem is that we don't know how to play football'.

West Ham United manager Sam Allardyce sounds like he's got some BIG problems to overcome

A goalkeeper once scored a hat-trick

We've heard of keepers scoring from their own goal kicks from time to time, and even a few keepers taking their turn during penalty shoot-outs, but has a goalkeeper really ever netted three times in the same game?

★ And the truth is...

You'd better believe it! The Paraguay international José Luis Chilavert was a free kick and penalty specialist, who scored a whopping 62 goals during his professional career, including eight in international matches. In fact, he scored four goals to help Paraguay qualify for the 2002 World Cup. Chilavert entered the record books in 1999, when he became the first goalkeeper to register a hat-trick, when he took – and scored – three penalties for his domestic side Véléz against Ferro Carril Oeste in the Argentinian league. He even once scored a free kick from behind the half-way line. Now that's just showing off.

Verdict:  TRUTH

FOOTBALL RECORD BREAKERS

No 2: The biggest loser

Paolo Maldini
....

Legendary Italian Paolo Maldini spend
25 years with AC Milan, collecting a
tear-jerking 17 runners-up medals
- making him the unluckiest man in
football. Maldini lost three Champions
League finals, three Intercontinental
/World Club Cups, two Coppa Italias,
three Supercoppas, a UEFA Super
Cup final, a World Cup final, and a
European Championship final and was
runner-up three times in the Italian
League. Phew.

David Beckham was England's dirtiest player

If you were asked to name a player who was always in trouble with the ref, chances are Beckham would be low down on the list. But rumour persists that he's the baddest boy ever to wear an England shirt.

★ And the truth is...

Beckham has won just about every major honour in the game. And one major dishonour. He is the only England player ever to be sent off twice. In 1998, during the World Cup in France, he was shown a red card for flailing a boot at Argentinian midfielder Diego Simeone. Then again in 2005 — and this time wearing the captain's armband — Beckham got his marching orders during a World Cup qualifier against Austria. All-time teacher's pet is Gary Lineker, who played 80 times for England, scoring 48 goals, and *was never even booked!*

Verdict:  TRUTH (ish)

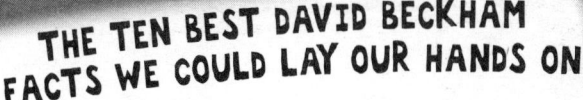

WELL I NEVER!

THE TEN BEST DAVID BECKHAM FACTS WE COULD LAY OUR HANDS ON

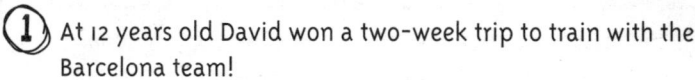

1. At 12 years old David won a two-week trip to train with the Barcelona team!

2. Elton John and Liz Hurley are godparents to David's children

3. David's legs were once insured for £43million

4. David suffers from ornithophobia, which is a fear of birds

5. David was the Professional Footballers' Association (PFA) Young Player of the Year in 1997

6. David has appeared in five films: *Goal I, II* and *III*, *Zidane: A 21st Century Portrait*, and *Real, The Movie*

7. Within 48 hours of announcing his signing to LA Galaxy, the club had sold more than 5,000 season tickets

8. With his goal against Ecuador during the 2006 World Cup, David became the first English player to score in three different World Cups

9. David has earned 115 England caps, a record number for an outfield player

10. David has won a league championship at all three of the clubs he has played for on a permanent basis: Manchester United, Real Madrid and LA Galaxy

God knocked England out of the 1986 World Cup

It's easy to believe that God isn't on England's side in World Cups, when you think of all the lost penalty shoot-outs. But we can't believe he's ever really pulled his boots on and played for the opposition.

⭐ And the truth is...

OK, it was Argentinian footballer Diego Maradona's handball against England, which he himself called 'the hand of God', that helped Argentina beat England 2-1 in the quarter-finals and send England home. The 1.6m (5ft 5in) Maradona out-jumped the 1.85m (6ft) England keeper Peter Shilton and punched the ball into the net. Amazingly, despite protests from the England team and bench, the referee allowed the goal to stand. Maradona later told reporters that the handball was revenge for Britain defeating Argentina in the Falklands War a few years earlier...

Verdict: A little bit true but mostly  BUSTED

THE BOY'S WORTH A FEW QUID!

Most expensive football transfers through the ages

DATE	PLAYER	FROM	TO	COST
1905	Alf Common	Sunderland	Middlesborough	£1,000
1922	Syd Puddefoot	West Ham Utd	Falkirk	£5,000
1952	Hans Jeppson	Atalanta	Napoli	£52,000
1968	Pietro Anastasi	Varese	Juventus	£500,000
1979	Trevor Francis	Birmingham City	Nottingham Forest	£1,000,000
1982	Diego Maradona	Boca Juniors	Barcelona	£3,000,000
1992	Jean-Pierre Papin	Marseille	Milan	£10,000,000
1996	Alan Shearer	Blackburn Rovers	Newcastle Utd	£15,000,000
1999	Christian Vieri	Lazio	Internazionale	£32,000,000
2001	Zinedine Zidane	Juventus	Real Madrid	£53,000,000
2009	Cristiano Ronaldo	Manchester Utd	Real Madrid	£80,000,000
2013	Gareth Bale	Tottenham Hotspur	Real Madrid	£85,000,000

A player once got THREE yellow cards before being sent off

We all know the drill — one yellow, you stay on. Second yellow, you're off for an early bath. Surely there are no exceptions to the rule?

And the truth is...

Well, it depends if the referee can count! During a World Cup match between Croatia and Australia in 2006, English referee Graham Poll gave Croatian defender Josip Šimunic his first yellow card in the 61st minute. In the 90th Šimunic found himself in the book again, but because of his Australian accent (Šimunic was actually born in Canberra), Poll took his name — wrongly — as 'Australian No 3' and *didn't* send him off. Only in the third minute of injury time, when Šimunic again went in the book for arguing, did Poll realise his mistake and finally give the Croatian his marching orders. The ref, who was favourite to referee the World Cup final, retired from international football straight after the game.

Verdict:  TRUTH

'WE LOST BECAUSE WE DIDN'T WIN'

The daftest football quotes collected

'The Germans only have one player under 22, and he's 23.'

Ex-England manager Kevin Keegan and former European Footballer of the Year proves that a lack of basic maths does not have to stand in the way of footballing success

'We nearly didn't sign him because the letters didn't fit on his shirt.'

Former Arsenal chairman on the signing of Dutch international Giovanni van Bronckhorst

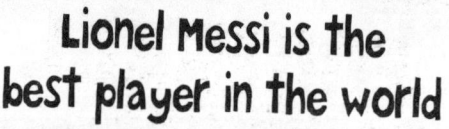

Lionel Messi is the best player in the world

MESSI OR MARTA ?

The tiny Argentinian wing wizard has won FIFA's World Player of the Year title an impressive five times. Can anyone beat that?

⭐ And the truth is...

Actually, there is someone who can at least match it. Her name is Marta Vieira da Silva and she is the most famous striker in the history of Brazilian women's football. Marta has matched Messi's five FIFA World Player of the Year titles — winning them consecutively from 2006-2010 (before she let someone else have a go). Marta, who wears the number 100 shirt, has scored over 80 times for her country and is regarded as the Messi of the female footballing world.

Verdict:  **BUSTED**

Peter Shilton

Ex-England goalkeeper Shilton holds the record for the most competitive games in world football with an impressive 1,390. During a 30-year professional career, he played for 11 different clubs, starting at Leicester City in 1966 and finishing at Leyton Orient in 1997. He also holds the record for England appearances with 125 caps.

The 2006 World cup caused a baby boom in Germany

How could it be that watching your national team could cause more babies to be born? Mmm, we're not buying it.

★ And the truth is...

In March 2007 20% more babies were born in Berlin (9 months after the World Cup) than in March 2006. The head of the largest birth clinic in the nearby city of Kassel, Rolf Kliche, estimated that births at his hospital were also up 10-15%. Kliche said he wasn't surprised 'because happiness tends to release hormones and makes it easier to get pregnant.'

And it's not just Germany where it's happening. Nine months after Barcelona's 2009 Champions League victory over Manchester United, Spanish maternity wards were reporting a whopping 45% increase in birth rate. In Barcelona, the babies are known as 'the Iniesta generation', after the striker who scored an injury time goal against Chelsea to put Barça through to the final.

Verdict: _____

SIX STRANGE SHIRT SPONSORS

FULHAM
– PIZZA HUT
(NOT EXACTLY PROMOTING HEALTHY EATING!)

AC MILAN
– POOH
(A TYPE OF JEANS)

LIVERPOOL FC
– CROWN PAINTS
(DECORATING ANYONE?)

PORTSMOUTH
– TY
(THE PEOPLE WHO MAKE BEANIE BABIES)

AS ROMA
– WIND
(AN ITALIAN MOBILE PHONE PROVIDER)

FC NURNBERG
– MISTER LADY
(A LOCAL CLOTHES SHOP FOR TEENS)

Yellow and red cards mimic traffic lights

Oh, we get it: yellow means stop (fouling your opponent) and red means really *really* stop — permanently! This sounds too far-fetched to be true.

★ And the truth is...

Before the invention of yellow cards, players could still be cautioned, but often didn't even know it had happened. In 1962, former referee Ken Ashton was driving home from work one day and was sitting at a set of traffic lights when he had a 'Eureka' moment — why not introduce a series of cards to show the players, officials and fans exactly what was going on?

FIFA introduced yellow and red cards in time for the 1970 World Cup in Mexico. In the opening game, Soviet defender Evgeny Lovchev went down in history as the first man to be shown a yellow card. Four other players went into the referee's book during that tournament, but no one was sent off.

Verdict:  TRUTH

'WE LOST BECAUSE WE DIDN'T WIN'

The daftest football quotes collected

'I definitely want (my son) Brooklyn to be christened, but I don't know into what religion yet.'

Officially the world's most famous footballer, David Beckham obviously didn't pay attention in his RS lessons

'Rooney was complaining all the time, protests and more protests. He reminded me of my kids.'

World Cup referee Horacio Elizondo puts Wayne Rooney straight

A footballer once drowned in a crocodile-infested river during training

Crikey, we knew pitches could get waterlogged and a bit hazardous but that's ridiculous. Is it true?

★ And the truth is...

Well, it's a little more complicated than a kickabout on a wet pitch. In 2009, the coach of Zimbabwean Division One side Midlands Portland Cement (catchy name!) took his 17-man squad down to the crocodile-infested Zambezi River for a 'spirit cleansing' exercise to force out evil spirits before a game against local rivals Sao Paolo. The players timidly splashed around the edges watched by the curious crocs, before paddling back to the bank to get dressed. On discovering a spare set of clothes left behind, the team realised that they had lost a player, whose body was sadly never found. Local officials believe he had been washed away by the river's strong currents. Gulp.

Verdict: ___ TRUTH ___

WEEING ON THE PITCH!

... AND OTHER WEIRD FOOTBALLING SUPERSTITIONS

France in the 1998 World Cup

The team's superstitions included always occupying the same seats on the team bus, listening to Gloria Gaynor's hit '*I Will Survive*' in the changing-room, and rounding it off with defender Laurent Blanc kissing goalkeeper Fabien Barthez's bald head before kick-off. France won the tournament so, hey, who's crazy after all?

Sergio Goycochea

The Argentinian goalkeeper used to wee on the pitch before facing a penalty. 'It was my lucky charm, and I did it before every shoot-out. Nobody complained,' he reckons. Well, we would have!

Bobby Moore

The World Cup-winning England captain always insisted on being the last person into the changing-room to put on his shorts before kick-off. Team-mate Martin Peters would wait until Moore had put on his shorts, then take his own off. Moore would then have to remove his shorts, and the whole thing started again...

Johan Cruyff

The Dutch legend used to land his goalkeeper a mock punch while he was at Ajax, and then spit his chewing gum into the opposition's half before kick-off (yuck!). When Cruyff once forgot his gum, in the European Cup final of 1969, Ajax lost to Milan 4-1.

A football match once turned into a war

We have seen how the odd football match can lead to a bit of bad feeling — on and off the pitch. But could it ever really lead to something more serious?
We need convincing!

And the truth is...

Strange as it sounds, a series of World Cup qualifying matches between Central American neighbours El Salvador and Honduras in 1969 led to an event known as the Soccer War.

There was more to it than a game of football, though. The two countries had been arguing about immigration policies for years. Honduras is over five times the size of El Salvador, but had half the population. So El Salvadorans were simply moving across the border and setting up farms on land that they had no legal right to. The Honduran government eventually expelled the Salvadoran settlers and redistributed the land, but left behind bad feeling between the two governments that threatened to boil over.

Against this backdrop, the two countries were drawn to play each other in qualifying for the 1970 World Cup in Mexico. The first game, which Honduras won 1-0, took place on 8 June 1969 and saw fighting between fans from both sides. The second game a week later finished 3-0 to El Salvador and led to police in the capital San Salvador struggling to regain order. And the final play-off match on 26 June was won 3-2 by El Salvador in extra time and led to the victors severing all diplomatic ties with Honduras, and closing its borders.

The El Salvadoran army and air force then launched surprise attacks on Honduras. Honduras retaliated with air raids of its own. Over 3,000 people were killed or wounded in a frantic four days of fighting, before pressure from the US and other South American governments persuaded the two countries to stop fighting and shake hands as friends. But after all these years, there are still problems between the two countries...

Verdict:

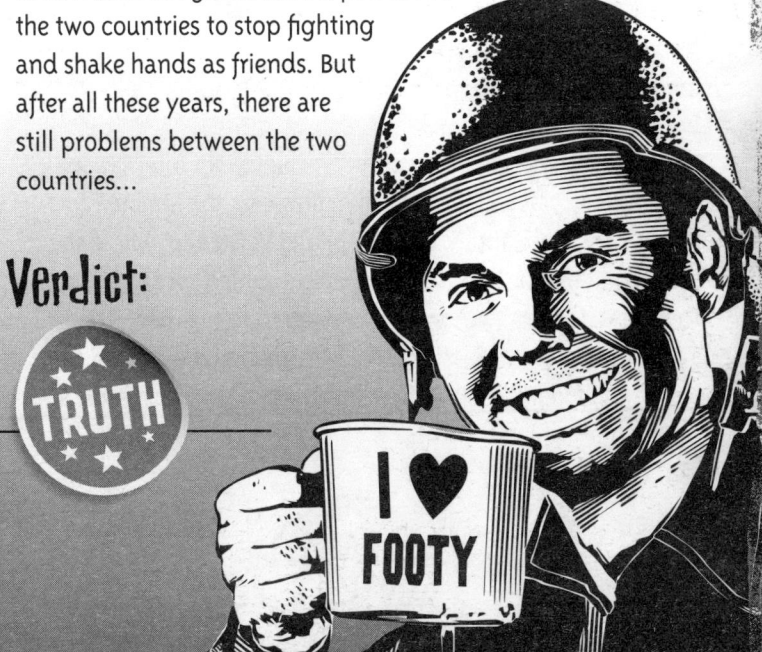

TRUTH

I ♥ FOOTY

The best ball juggler in the world is female

'Check this out chaps!'

We've never been any good at keepie-uppie, so we're prepared to believe anything here.

★ And the truth is...

Brazilian footballer Milene Domingues holds the world record for ball juggling with a mind-boggling 55,198 touches (who exactly was keeping count?!). The former international, now retired, played her football in Brazil for the famous Corinthians club, and in Spain for Rayo Vallecano, where she set a women's transfer record when she joined for £200,000. Though it doesn't sound much compared to the men, it was a tidy sum in the women's game. Oh, and Milene used to be married to legendary Brazilian striker Ronaldo — so maybe she taught him a thing or two!

Verdict: _____ TRUTH

A goalkeeper once dislocated his jaw shouting at his teammates

You can often see goalkeepers shouting at their defenders when they're trying to organise them at corners and free kicks. But do they ever injure themselves trying to get the words out?

'Arghhhhh!'

 And the truth is...

Manchester United goalkeeper Alex Stepney played alongside the likes of George Best and Bobby Charlton, and helped win the European Cup for the reds in 1968. He played over 400 times for United and once had the misfortune of conceding a goal direct from the opposing team's goal kick. What's not so well known about the fearsome shot stopper is that he once got so hot under the collar with his defenders during a game against Birmingham City in 1975, that he dislocated his jaw and ended up in A&E.

Verdict:

(Turn the page for more crazy football injuries!)

THE WORLD'S ODDEST FOOTBALL INJURIES

YOU COULDN'T MAKE THESE UP. SO WE DIDN'T - THEY ARE ALL 100% TRUE!

DAVE BEASANT - JAR OF SALAD CREAM

The veteran Wimbledon goalkeeper managed to rule himself out for eight weeks in 1993 when he dropped a bottle of salad cream on his bare foot, severing the tendon in his big toe.

MILAN RAPAIC - AIRLINE BOARDING PASS

The Croatian international missed the start of the season for Hadjuk Split when he accidentally stuck his boarding-pass in his eye at the airport on the way to a pre-season tour.

KASEY KELLER - GOLF CLUBS

The American international goalkeeper knocked out his front teeth while pulling his golf clubs out of the boot of his car.

DARREN BARNARD - PUPPY PEE

The former UK team Barnsley's midfielder was sidelined for five months with a torn knee ligament after he slipped in a puddle of his puppy's wee on the kitchen floor.

DAVID JAMES – TV REMOTE
The former England goalkeeper once pulled a muscle in his back while reaching for the TV remote control.

PAOLO DIOGO – WEDDING RING
The Swiss midfielder jumped over advertising hoardings in December 2004 to celebrate a winning goal. Unfortunately, he caught his wedding ring on the perimeter fence and tore off the top half of his finger! Ouch

RIO FERDINAND – COFFEE TABLE
During his spell at Leeds, the England and Manchester Utd defender sat in front of the TV with his feet on a coffee table for so long that he ended up injuring a tendon behind his knee.

DAVID BATTY – TODDLER
The former Leeds and Blackburn midfielder injured his Achilles tendon when he was run over by his toddler on a tricycle.

STEVE MORROW – PIGGYBACK
The former Northern Ireland defender broke his collarbone after falling off the shoulders of a teammate while celebrating the 1993 League Cup final victory.

SVEIN GRØNDALEN – MOOSE
The veteran Norway defender had to withdraw from an international during the 1970s after colliding with a moose while out jogging.

Footballers earn less than their underpants do

This one needs a little bit of explaining. What we mean is that, by modelling for underwear brands like Armani and H&M, pin-up footballers like Cristiano Ronaldo and David Beckham earn more in advertising revenue than they do from playing football. You see, it's not such a daft statement after all…

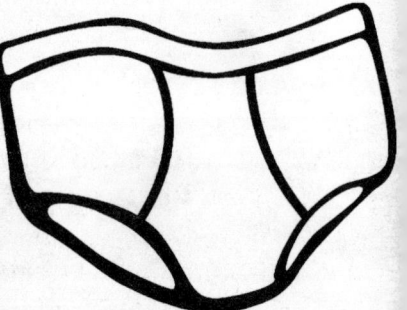

★ And the truth is…

Well, let's start with what we know or can at least estimate. It's been claimed that, in 2012, Becks and Ronaldo earned a rather handsome £26.2m and £24.3m respectively. But, how much of that was salary from their clubs? In Beck's case, it was £1.84m (not sure how he makes ends meet?), and with Ronaldo a whopping £10.6m. So we can deduce, as Sherlock Holmes would say, that for the two gentlemen in question, their underpants are indeed the main breadwinners. Amazing!

Verdict: **TRUTH**

FOOTBALLERS' EARNINGS

— 1901 —
Wage limit of £4 per week

— 1922 —
Maximum wage rises to £8 per week (£6 in the summer)

— 1979 —
Nottingham Forest goalkeeper Peter Shilton is the best-paid player in Britain with a salary of £1,200 per week

— 2001 —
Defender Sol Campbell's move from Tottenham to Arsenal makes his the first £100,000 per week player in the Premiership

— 2009 —
Cristiano Ronaldo joins Real Madrid from Manchester United. His wages are a whopping £180,000 per week

— 2010 —
Carlos Tevez becomes the first £1m per month player, with estimated wages of £286,000 per week at Manchester City

— 2013 —
Lionel Messi is the highest paid player in the world, with wages of over £500,000 per week at Barcelona (equivalent to an annual salary of £27.5m)

Early footballers used a pig's bladder instead of a ball

The modern football is an aerodynamic masterpiece that can bend around walls and win World Cup finals. But a pig's bladder? Yeeeww, surely not?

★ And the truth is...

Guilty as charged! Early footballs were made of leather but contained an inflated pig's or cow's bladder. But that's not so weird when you learn that before inflated pigs' bladders, keen footballers used to kick around anything from a stitched-up bag of rags to a human head! The use of pigs' bladders started in the Middle Ages, but later the leather outer shell was added to avoid punctures...

Verdict:  _____

FOOTBALL RECORD BREAKERS

Pelé
. . . .

Edison Arantes do Nascimento (to give him his full name) was a footballing phenomenon, regarded by many people as the greatest player of all time. He is certainly the top scorer, with a mind-boggling 1,281 career goals in just 1,363 games (that's a goal every 95 minutes!) Pelé is also Brazil's top scorer with 77 goals, and is the only player to be part of three World Cup-winning teams.

The stolen 1966 World Cup trophy was found by a dog called Pickles

The story is quite well known — scruffy mongrel saves England's embarrassment when it discovers the stolen World Cup trophy under a bush. But is it fact or fiction?

And the truth is...

In March 1966, the famous Jules Rimet trophy went on display in England, before the World Cup that summer. It was promptly stolen (had no one heard of burglar alarms?) and not long afterwards a petty thief called Edward Walter Bletchley contacted the police and demanded £15,000 in used notes to return it. Bletchley was promptly arrested.

Police were baffled, and plans were put in place to make a bronze replica of the trophy, just in case the original couldn't be found. Thankfully, just one week later, the trophy was discovered in a front garden in south London by Dave Corbett, who was out walking his dog, Pickles. However, Dave refused to give his pet any of the credit for the find: 'Although Pickles sort of led me in [the right direction], it was me who found it. There were all these stories... that he dug it up from under a bush, [but that didn't happen].'

What did happen, is that Dave received an award of £6,000 for finding the trophy — six times the amount the England team got for winning it — and Pickles received a year's supply of dog food. Even though his owner claims he did nothing to earn it — the hairy scrounger!

Verdict:

> # A fan was banned for swinging a dead chicken around his head to celebrate a goal

Fans — and players — do the strangest things to celebrate goals (see opposite page), but dead fowl? Surely not.

★ And the truth is...

Manchester City fans fondly remember one of their number arriving at a game in 1995 with his (uncooked) Sunday dinner in a shopping bag, ready to take home and eat after the match. They also clearly remember him waving the plucked, featherless bird around his head to celebrate a winning goal. Rumour has it that when parts of the bird started flying off, and landing in fellow supporters' laps, the fan was politely asked to put his chicken away. Even more bizarrely, the trend caught on and for the rest of the season, several like-minded fans celebrated with the help of joke shop rubber chickens! And was the fan banned for his, erm, fowl behaviour? Apparently not!

Verdict:  **BUSTED**

THE WORLD'S BEST GOAL CELEBRATIONS

WHY? BECAUSE WE LOVE THEM!

Peter Crouch - robot
UK's Sunderland striker Crouch become known for his robotic dance moves in the pre-tournament friendlies before the 2006 World Cup, celebrating goals against Hungary and Jamaica with a freaky robotic dance.

Facundo Sava - mask
The Argentinian striker pulled on a black face mask and ran to supporters to celebrate each of his seven goals during his two-year stay at Fulham.

Bebeto - baby
After scoring against Holland in the 1994 World Cup quarter-finals, the Brazilian striker ran to the side of the pitch and started to rock an imaginary baby. His wife had given birth just a few days before, in case you wondered.

Edmilson Ferreira - carrot
A striker with Brazilian club Atletico Mineiro, Ferreira celebrated scoring a goal against neighbours America-Belo Horizonte - nicknamed the Rabbits - by pulling a carrot out of his shorts and eating it!

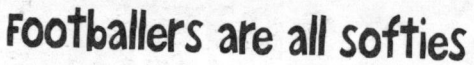
Footballers are all softies

We've all seen it — falling over, clutching at their ankles, anything to get a free kick. Not to mention playing in gloves. In April! Surely footballers are the biggest softies in sport?

'And the winner is...'

⭐ And the truth is...

Yes, they do tend to fall down and roll around a lot more these days (and wrap up against the cold — bless), but footballers must be tough. The evidence? Manchester City goalkeeper Bert Trautmann actually broke his neck while playing for Manchester City in the 1956 FA Cup Final — and played on to the end of the game! Spectators at the time thought Trautmann's neck looked a bit wonky when he went up to collect his medal, but the courageous German didn't even go to the hospital until three days later, when the injury was finally revealed!

Verdict: **BUSTED**

FOOTBALL RECORD BREAKERS

No 5: The most World Cup wins

Brazil
....

The team in the familiar gold shirts and green shorts have won the World Cup a record-breaking five times, and are also the only team to appear in every tournament to date. Victories came in 1958, 1962, 1970, 1994 and 2002. When they completed a hat-trick of victories in 1970, they were allowed to keep the Jules Rimet Trophy permanently!

The world's highest scoring international player is a woman

Think about the great goal scorers and who comes to mind? Pelé for Brazil, David Villa for Spain. We weren't even thinking of a woman. But we should...

★ And the truth is...

Former US international Mia Hamm blows all those goalscorers out of the water, with an eye-watering 158 goals for her country! That's nearly as many as Pelé (77), Drogba (59) and Džeko (26) put together. Mia (short for Mariel Margaret) won the Women's World Cup with USA in 1999, scoring the winning goal in the penalty shoot-out against China. She played for her country a huge 275 times over a 17-year period from 1987-2004 and, amazingly, was born with a club foot — and had to wear corrective shoes as a toddler. Mia is so famous in the USA that Nike named a whole building after her at their Oregon headquarters.

Verdict: _____ TRUTH _____

'WE LOST BECAUSE WE DIDN'T WIN'

The daftest football quotes collected

'I've learned that you have to score goals to win games.'

Ex-Valencia and Liverpool manager, and Champions League winner, Rafa Benitez, obviously knows what he's talking about

'They're the second best team in the world, and there's no higher praise than that.'

Ex-England manager Kevin Keegan can't quite put his finger on it

A football team was once threatened with death if they lost

Blimey, we're heard about the 'hairdryer' treatment from a manager at half-time, but death threats? Wouldn't want to be in that dressing room!

★ And the truth is...

In 1980, the tiny West African nation of Liberia was involved in a bloody civil war. The army, led by Master Sergeant Samuel Doe, overthrew and killed the President William Tolbert and most of his government. Doe ruled the country for nine years, regularly fixing elections to keep himself in power. Doe was obviously a man who didn't take no for an answer. He was also a football fan and, gulp, made it clear to the Liberian national team that if they lost to Gambia in a forthcoming international, he would personally suffer huge embarrassment — and *they* would all face the firing squad. Luckily Liberia drew the game!

Verdict:

48

FOOTBALL RECORD BREAKERS

Francisco Gento
....

The little-known left-winger played for an all-conquering Real Madrid side from 1953 until his retirement in 1971, collecting a record-breaking six European Cups, 12 Spanish league titles and two Spanish Cups. This makes him the most successful player that no one has ever heard of!

A Scottish footballer once won an Oscar

Footballers have occasionally appeared in films but their acting skills are usually more believable when they're diving to win a penalty. Could a player ever be Oscar-worthy?

⭐ And the truth is...

Yes! James Edmund Neil Paterson did it with a typewriter! Paterson joined the Scottish team Dundee United in 1936 and quickly became captain. After the Second World War, however, he never returned to the game and concentrated on a writing career. Paterson started writing novels and won several awards. One of his stories was turned into a film *The Kidnappers* in 1953, and after that he switched to writing screenplays himself. Amazingly, in 1959 he won an Oscar for the screenplay of a film called *Room At The Top*, based on a best-selling novel. Back of the net!

Verdict:  _____

'WE LOST BECAUSE WE DIDN'T WIN'

The daftest football quotes collected

'This is an unusual Scottish side because they have good players.'

→ Spanish coach Javier Clemente praises his Scottish opponents. Or does he?

'(The manager) said just two words to me in six months - you're fired!'

→ Swedish international striker Tomas Brolin wasn't on his manager's Christmas list — or team list...

Cristiano Ronaldo was named after US president Ronald Reagan

Cristiano Ronaldo dos Santos Aveiro, to give him his full name, is one of the best-known footballers on the planet. Named after an old American President? We doubt it.

⭐ And the truth is...

You'd better believe it! Ronaldo was given the name by his late father, José, because the US President was José's favourite Hollywood actor. Yes, Ronald Reagan had once been a Hollywood star in the 1940s and 1950s, appearing in films like *Cattle Queen of Montana*, and *Bedtime For Bonzo* (in which he co-starred with a chimpanzee) before moving into politics. It's clear that Ronaldo's dad had no taste in actors, but at least he knew how to spot a good footballer!

Verdict: _____ **TRUTH** _____

THE STRANGE NAMES XI

TWO-BOYS GUMEDE
South Africa

CHRIST BONGO
Democratic
Republic of Congo

JOHNNY MOUSTACHE
Seychelles

GERNOT SICK
Austria

DIETER STINKA
Germany

ZOLTAN KISS
Hungary

RAZVAN RAT
Romania

HARRY DAFT
England

GARETH JELLYMAN
Wales

DANIEL KILLER
Argentina

**GOALKEEPER:
NORMAN CONQUEST**
Australia

(and they're all real!)

A game once ended with only two players left on the field

The laws of the game state that football teams cannot play with less than seven players a side. That means a referee could show the red card eight times and still continue with a match. But 20 times in one game? Impossible.

★ And the truth is...

There have been several occasions when a fight on the pitch has led to a referee showing ten or more red cards, and therefore abandoning a game. As recently as 2009, a Spanish ref showed 19 reds in a match between two lower divisions sides after a mass brawl. But the world record is indeed 20 red cards. The incident occurred in a Paraguayan league match between Sportivo Ameliano and General Caballero. When two Sportivo players were sent off, punches were thrown, a 10-minute fight ensued and the referee dismissed a further 18 players. The match, not surprisingly, was abandoned.

Verdict:  TRUTH

'WE LOST BECAUSE WE DIDN'T WIN'

The daftest football quotes collected

'There are two great teams in Liverpool: Liverpool and Liverpool Reserves.'

Former Liverpool manager Bill Shankly doesn't think much of fellow Merseysiders Everton

'When you score one goal more than the other team in a cup tie it is always enough.'

Former Italy coach Cesare Maldini explains why he's qualified to be a football manager

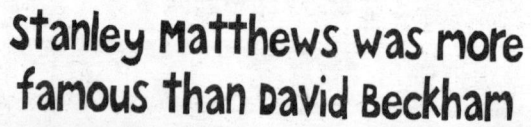

Stanley Matthews was more famous than David Beckham

Surprisingly for a man called Stanley (and playing for Blackpool!), Matthews was the pin-up of his day. But did he really trump Mr Beckham for all-round hero status?

★ And the truth is...

Stanley Matthews was a footballing superstar. He electrified football fans around the country with his Ronaldo-esque dribbling skills, played professional football for a jaw-dropping 33 years (that's even longer than Ryan Giggs!) and was knighted while still playing professionally. On top of that, he won the first ever European Footballer of the Year award (in 1956), and was so famous that when his team mate Stan Mortensen (were there no other names in the 1950s?) scored a hat-trick in the 1953 FA Cup Final to help Blackpool beat Bolton Wanderers 4-3, it still became known as the Matthews Final, as Stan provided the cross for the winning goal. Beat that, Becks!

Verdict: ——— TRUTH ———

THE WIZARD OF THE DRIBBLE

Fun facts about England's greatest footballer

Stan's father was a featherweight boxer nicknamed The Fighting Barber. That's because he was also a barber

At 17, Stan turned professional with Stoke City on wages of £5 per week (£3 in the summer)

Stan played for England for a whopping 23 years from 1934-1957

When Stan eventually retired from professional football at 50 years old in 1965, 100 million people watched his final game on TV

Stan's diet was the same every day of his playing career - carrot juice for lunch, steak with salad for dinner, and a fast on Mondays

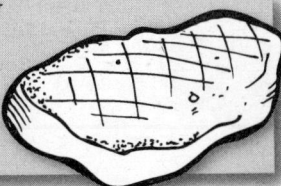

One of Stan's children, Stanley Jr (we're not making this up), won the Wimbledon Junior Championships in 1962

A club's mascot was shown the red card

Come on, ref! Those fluffy owls, wolves and dragons with the oversize heads never did anyone any harm. Or did they?

RED CARD

★ And the truth is...

You'd better believe it! The mascot at Bury FC, Robbie the Bobby (who is actually dressed as a policeman) was 'sent off' three times in as many months during the 2001-02 season. Twice for what the referee described as 'over-exuberant goal celebrations' (we're not sure he could have got his shirt over his large head and policeman's helmet?) and once for a spat with Welsh Cardiff City mascot, Barclay the Bluebird!

Verdict:  TRUTH

FOOTBALL RECORD BREAKERS

Pedro Ribeiro Lima

The Brazilian midfielder is still playing for Desportiva Perilima (a team he founded himself) at the ripe old age of 58. The sporting granddad starting turning out for his team, who play in the Brazilian regional first division, when he thought the team needed his help!

HMMPH

THE INCREDIBLE
SULK

THE INCREDIBLE SULK...
AND OTHER GREAT PLAYERS' NICKNAMES

NICOLAS ANELKA (FRANCE) – THE INCREDIBLE SULK
The striker earned his nickname during a two-year spell at Arsenal, when he spent the whole time wandering around looking fed up

ALJOŠA ASANOVIĐ (CROATIA) – THE FIERY ELBOW
The midfielder has a reputation for running with his arms out and 'accidentally' elbowing opponents

FERENC PUSKÁS (HUNGARY) – THE GALLOPING MAJOR
The legendary Real Madrid striker played for the Hungarian army and held the honorary rank of major

FITZ HALL (ENGLAND) – ONE SIZE

One size Fitz Hall, geddit? The Watford defender has carried his wonderful nickname for over a decade since some bright spark dreamed it up while he was playing for Oldham

ROBERTO BAGGIO (ITALY) – THE DIVINE PONYTAIL

Yes, before you ask, he did have a ponytail. He also missed a penalty that lost Italy the 1994 World Cup Final

LIONAL MESSI (ARGENTINA) – THE ATOMIC FLEA

The Barcelona whizz kid is fast, small and makes his home in cats' fur. OK, only the first two facts are true

CHORTLE

JULIO BAPTISTA (BRAZIL) – THE BEAST

We don't think he actually was a beast, but he was built like one

A goalkeeper once won six medals without playing a game

Hang on a minute, we didn't think you could get a trophy for carrying the drinks at half-time. How did that happen?

★ And the truth is...

Current German ladies international goalkeeper Nadine Angerer is pretty amazing. She holds the record for clean sheets in a World Cup — keeping the ball out of her net for a whopping 540 minutes (including a penalty save in the final) when Germany won the 2007 Women's World Cup. What's less well known about Nadine is that for almost ten years she kept the German bench warm as reserve keeper to Silke Rottenberg. Germany won the 2003 Women's World Cup, bronze medals at the 2000 and 2004 Olympics and three European Championships in 1997, 2001 and 2005 — and Nadine never touched the ball once!

Verdict: _____ TRUTH _____

FOOTBALL RECORD BREAKERS

Roberto Trotta
••••••••••••••••••••

This retired Argentinian defender, who played in the Spanish, Italian, Argentinian and Mexican leagues during an 18-year professional career holds the record for the most red cards with an embarrassing 17!

> # The FA Cup Final is always played at Wembley

OK smarty pants, we all know that from 2001-2006, Cup Finals were played at Cardiff's Millennium Stadium while Wembley was being rebuilt. We mean apart from that. So... is this statement fact or fiction?

★ And the truth is...

We bet you didn't know that from 1893 to 1914, Cup Finals were played at Crystal Palace in South London. At this time, Wembley hadn't even been built, and finals were played anywhere from Sheffield, to Manchester to Liverpool to name but three. When the FA decided that Cup Finals needed to move permanently to London, Crystal Palace was the obvious choice — the Victorian park grounds held a grand football stadium and a shiny all-glass exhibition centre that gave the area its name. Off the wall fact: Crystal Palace, the club, has at the time of writing never won the coveted trophy. Although they were runners-up to Manchester United in 1990, when they lost in a replay. At Wembley.

Verdict: BUSTED

'WE LOST BECAUSE WE DIDN'T WIN'

The daftest football quotes collected

'Of the nine red cards this season we probably deserved half of them.'

Ah, this explains why Arsenal manager Arsène Wenger is nicknamed 'The Professor'

'The best Italian this club has signed is the chef.'

Former French international, and Chelsea defender, Frank Leboeuf obviously didn't rate his Italian teammates Luca Vialli, Roberto di Matteo or Gianfranco Zola

Newcastle United inspired the windscreen wiper

The sight of a full team of strapping lads in black and white striped shirts may have inspired many things but did it really bring about a truly game-changing invention for the automobile industry?

★ And the truth is...

Steps back in amazement, but yes it's true. In 1908, Newcastle fan Gladstone Adams drove down to Crystal Palace to watch his beloved Magpies get beaten 3-1 by Wolves in the FA Cup Final. To add insult to injury, on the long drive back up north, Gladstone had to keep stopping his rather swish French-built Darracq car to clear snow and slush off his windscreen. The frustrating journey inspired him to invent windscreen wipers, which he patented in 1911. Newcastle could do with some of Gladstone's inventiveness now — they haven't won the FA Cup since 1955!

Verdict:  TRUTH

FOOTBALL RECORD BREAKERS

No 9: The shortest international player

Frederick 'Fanny' Walden

This pocket-sized 1.57m (5ft 2in) winger (that's the same height as an average 13-year-old girl) played for Tottenham Hotspur before the First World War and won two England caps. Which were probably too big for him...

Footballers used to be some of the lowest-paid workers in the country

Penny for the footballer?

Cristiano Ronaldo and Lionel Messi seem to earn about a million pounds a minute. And Manchester City players aren't too far behind. So could footballers ever have been hard up? Sounds unlikely.

★ And the truth is...

You wouldn't think so these days, but back in the late 19th century, footballers were a relatively hard-up bunch. In 1893, clubs introduced a maximum wage of £4 per week to stop their best players being poached by wealthier clubs. In 1910, this was raised — to £5! By 1959, it had climbed to £20 during the season, dropping to £14 a week during the summer, when everyone knows that footballers put their feet up on the sun lounger and read the paper. Average wages at the time were around £14, so footballers earned the equivalent of a factory worker. Maybe that should happen today too! (For more information, flip back to page 36-7.)

Verdict: _____ TRUTH _____

'WE LOST BECAUSE WE DIDN'T WIN'

The daftest football quotes collected

'I always used to put my right boot on first, and then obviously my right sock.'

Former Newcastle United captain Barry Venison explains his weird pre-match superstition. Very weird

'Alex Ferguson is the best manager I've ever had at this level. Well, he's the only manager I've actually had at this level...'

Global superstar David Beckham explains his love and respect for Manchester United Alex Ferguson, while he was still playing at Old Trafford

The penalty kick was invented by an Irish factory owner

Who was responsible for one of the most groundbreaking rules of football? Surely a bigwig in the game who realised it would add drama — and a sense of fairness — to the beautiful game.

⭐ And the truth is...

Nope, it was a bloke in Ireland who ran his millionaire father's linen mill, and played in goal for the local team at the weekend! William McCrum was an enthusiastic amateur keeper, who got tired of the chaos in his penalty area during every game, with defenders hacking down forwards to stop them scoring at all costs. In 1890 he proposed the penalty kick as 'the ultimate sanction' against a player making an illegal tackle. Football authorities thought it was a great idea, and adopted it in time for the 1891-92 season. And England have been regretting the decision ever since!

Verdict: **TRUTH**

FOOTBALL RECORD BREAKERS

Pep Guardiola

There are a few men with a claim to this title, but we're going for former Barcelona manager Pep Guardiola – the only man to lead a team to an incredible six trophies in one year! During 2009, his Barcelona side won the Spanish league, the Copa del Rey, the Champions League, the Spanish Super Cup, the UEFA Super Cup and, finally, the FIFA Club World Cup!

The USA are the best football team in the world

Aren't you thinking of basketball? We know the US are brilliant at most things, but football — or should we say soccer? Erm, not so sure about that.

★ And the truth is...

Who said we were talking about men's football? The US women's national team put their male counterparts to shame, and are the most successful national team in women's football by a mile. They won the first Women's World Cup in 1991, and have never looked back, racking up a second World Cup win in 1999, four Olympic gold medals in 1996, 2004, 2008 and 2012 and eight Algarve Cups (the equivalent of an international Champions League) between 2000-2011. Not bad for a team that only played its first international in 1985!

Verdict: _____ TRUTH _____

'WE LOST BECAUSE WE DIDN'T WIN'

The daftest football quotes collected

'The Dutch side look like a huge jar of marmalade.'

Commentator Barry Davies wants to take a bite out of Holland's tasty orange kit

'A little bit the hand of God, a little the head of Diego.'

Argentinian striker Diego Maradona describes his hotly disputed goal against England at the 1986 World Cup finals

MATCH THE FOOTBALL

The Boleyn Ground, England

Georgios Karaiskakis Stadium, Greece

Donbass Arena, Ukraine

Estadio Da Luz (Stadium of Light), Portugal

Stadium of Light, England

Soccer City, South Africa

Westfalenstadion, Germany

Sports Direct Arena, England

La Bombonera, Argentina

Luzhniki Stadium, Russia

Vicente Calderon, Spain

Mestalla Stadium, Spain

Camp Nou, Spain

Mercedes Benz Arena, Germany

Atlético Madrid

Olympiakos

Portugal – Benfica

Shakhtar Donetsk

Boca Juniors

VfB Stuttgart

Borussia Dortmund

Sunderland

CSKA Moscow and Spartak Moscow

Newcastle United

FC Barcelona

West Ham United (also known as Upton Park)

Kaiser Chiefs

Valencia

Answers:

The Boleyn Ground, (also known as Upton Park) **England** — West Ham United.
Georgios Karaiskakis Stadium, Greece — Olympiakos. **Mercedes Benz Arena, Germany** — VfB Stuttgart.
Vicente Calderon, Spain — Atletico Madrid. **Stadium of Light, England** — Sunderland.
Sports Direct Arena, England — Newcastle United. **Donbass Arena, Ukraine** — Shakhtar Donetsk.
Luzhniki Stadium, Russia — CSKA Moscow and Spartak Moscow. **Mestalla Stadium, Spain** — Valencia.
Camp Nou, Spain — FC Barcelona. **La Bombonera, Argentina** — Boca Juniors.
Westfalenstadion, Germany — Borussia Dortmund. **Soccer City, South Africa** — Kaiser Chiefs.
Estadio Da Luz (Stadium of Light), Portugal — Benfica.

Footballers used to wear cricket pads instead of shin pads

There are several footballers who have also represented their country at cricket, but surely they didn't wear the same kit for both sports?!

★ And the truth is...

Nottingham Forest centre forward Sam Widdowson invented the ankle-saving safety measure back in 1874. But he went a bit Superman on it. Tired of getting kicked in the shins by over-enthusiastic opponents, Widdowson cut down a pair of cricket pads *and wore them over the top of his socks*. Team mates and opponents fell about laughing at the sight of his weird white shin protectors, but before long every player in the league was wearing Widdowson's invention. Then one bright spark realised they would look better *inside* his socks, and the rest is history!

Verdict:  TRUTH

FOOTBALL RECORD BREAKERS

Hungary
....

Strange though it might sound, the Hungarian national team are easily the most successful in Olympic history with a haul of three gold medals, one silver and one bronze. Striker Ferenc Bene scored an incredible 12 goals at the 1964 tournament, including the winning goal in the final.

A school headmaster invented football

Most headmasters are too busy handing out detention, and nipping in at the front of the lunch queue to do anything really useful. Did one of them really invent the world's favourite game?

★ And the truth is...

As head of St Paul's school in London during the late 16th century, Richard Mulcaster didn't exactly *invent* football but he almost single-handedly popularised the game in Britain, and shaped it from a free-for-all kick about to an organised team sport. He pushed for football's inclusion in the school curriculum, believing it promoted pupils' health and fitness, and also helped introduce referees, playing positions and even a coach to the game, which he named the 'trayning master'. His spelling wasn't up to much, but we can't fault his intentions!

Verdict: <u>(mostly)</u> 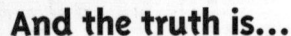 TRUTH

'We are happy with the three points, but it could have been more.'

Manchester United legend Ryan Giggs is never satisfied. No Ryan, we think you'll find it couldn't have been more

'Cristiano Ronaldo has a left foot, a right foot - the list is endless.'

Former Manchester United player Steve Coppell shows that he can count up Ronaldo's feet

JUMPERS FOR GOALPOSTS

The world's greatest football inventions

Shirt numbers

Numbers were first worn on shirts in an English First Division match between Arsenal and Sheffield Wednesday on 25 August 1928. In 2005, Sao Paolo goalkeeper Rogério Ceni (see page 9) wore the highest-ever shirt number, 618, to commemorate a record-breaking number of appearances for the club.

Floodlights

Battery-powered lights date back as far as 1878, when Darwen FC and Sheffield started using them to illuminate gloomy winter games. The first international game played under floodlights was England versus Spain at Wembley, which England won 4-1.

Referee's whistle

There is some mystery surrounding the first use of a ref's whistle in a game. We know it was the 1870s, but historians debate where it was 1874 or 1878. Before the introduction of a whistle, referees indicated their decisions by waving a handkerchief, which is, frankly, daft.

Crossbar

The Football Association introduced the wooden crossbar in 1875, replacing tape that had previously marked the top of the goal. Rules stated that the crossbar should be 8ft (2.4m) above the ground. So no one except Peter Crouch would bang their head on it.

Substitutes

As early as the 1860s, subs were allowed to replace players who didn't turn up for a game. The modern substitute was introduced from the 1965-66 season in England, with one sub allowed per team, but only to replace an injured player. By the 1965-66 season, subs were allowed for tactical reasons – for example, if someone was having a bad game.

Linesmen

Early football matches were officiated by two 'umpires', one provided by each team. By the 1880s, a referee was added to keep time and settle arguments between the teams. Whenever a disagreement arose, umpires would refer to this official – hence the name 'referee'. By 1891, the referee had been moved on to the field of play and the umpires moved off the pitch to become linesmen.

Penalty shoot-out

Israeli Yosef Dagan is credited with inventing the penalty shoot out after watching his national team lose a 1968 Olympic quarter-final by drawing lots. The idea was endorsed by FIFA as early as 1970. Cue nail-biting finishes to every important England game since!

Football boots

Believe it or not, Henry VIII owned the world's first pair of football boots, way back in 1525. They were made by his personal shoemaker, Cornelius Johnson, at a cost of 4 shillings (the equivalent of £100 in today's money). No trace of the boots remains, unfortunately, but the Royal footwear is known to have been made of strong leather, ankle high and heavier than the normal shoe of the day. Fancy a kick about, Henry?

> # David Beckham hasn't always played at the top level

Did Tom Cruise's best mate ever turn out for a team with about as much star-power as a 30-watt light bulb? Phew, we doubt it!

★ And the truth is...

Indeed he did! The man they call Becks made five appearances for Preston North End during the 1994/95 season. He was only 19 at the time, and Manchester United manager Alex Ferguson believed the Cockney winger would benefit from some first team action. And so he did. Two typical Becks' goals — one from a free kick, and one direct from a corner, persuaded Fergie to bring him back to Old Trafford sharpish and throw him in at the deep end with United legends like Eric Cantona and Mark Hughes. Becks never looked back, playing 394 times for the club and winning six Premiership titles, two FA Cups and a Champions League medal. And all thanks to Preston!

Verdict: TRUTH

FOOTBALL RECORD BREAKERS

No 12: The most expensive football programme

Manchester United vs Bristol City

In May 2012 a single-sheet programme from the 1909 FA Cup Final was sold for a world-record £23,500 at Sotheby's in London. It beat the previous record of £21,850 for the 1889 Cup Final between Wolves and Preston.

> ## Italian champions Juventus adopted their kit from UK club Notts County

Sorry? One of the greatest clubs in football borrows its trademark black and white stripes from the soccer powerhouse that is… Notts County?

★ And the truth is…

Sometimes you have to believe the unbelievable. The 28-time Italian champions were formed in 1897 as Sport Club Juventus, and joined the Italian League in 1900. At this time, the club wore a frankly bizarre kit of pink shirts and black shorts. The club president Alfredo Dick obviously felt his team needed something more eye-catching. As luck would have it, he had a close friend living in Nottingham who was a big Notts Country supporter. The friend suggested Dick's men switch to his own team's bold black and white tops, and even sent over a consignment of said jerseys to the boys in Turin. Hey presto, the Italian *bianconeri* (that's 'white and blacks' to us) were born!

Verdict: **TRUTH**

'WE LOST BECAUSE WE DIDN'T WIN'

The daftest football quotes collected

'I am a Nigerian and I will remain a Nigerian until the day I die.'

→ Patriotic striker Kanu who is, we think, Nigerian

'A handball is when your hand touches the ball.'

→ Commentator Gary Lineker explains why he's qualified to explain the rules of the game on television

JOSÉ Mourinho used to work
as a manager's translator

Did the self-proclaimed 'best manager in the game' start his
career translating someone else's words, rather than spouting
his own gems? We can't imagine that one.

★ And the truth is...

Well, believe it or not, it happened. Mourinho was an
average player who failed to make it as a professional,
but was determined to follow his father into a football
management career. When ex-England boss Bobby Robson
joined Portuguese side Sporting Lisbon in 1992 as manager,
an enterprising Mourinho applied to work alongside him,
translating the Englishman's words into Portuguese. Mourinho
followed Robson to FC Porto in 1994, and then Spanish legends
Barcelona in 1996, by which time the Portuguese 'special one'
was developing his own coaching skills with the Barcelona B
team. In 2000, he made the switch to management full-time.

Verdict: _____ TRUTH _____

A player was sent off for impersonating himself

Hang on, we don't even understand this one. If he wasn't himself, then who was he? Or was he himself, but just pretending? Or...

⭐ And the truth is...

It's actually much simpler than it sounds. And it has a lot to do with a referee's sense-of-humour failure. In April 2011, Brazilian wonderkid striker Neymar was playing for his club Santos against Chilean side Colo Colo in the Copa Libertadores (the South American version of the Champions League). When Neymar scored a superb individual winning goal,

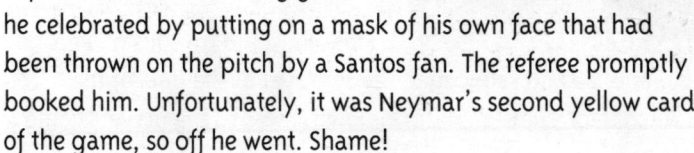

he celebrated by putting on a mask of his own face that had been thrown on the pitch by a Santos fan. The referee promptly booked him. Unfortunately, it was Neymar's second yellow card of the game, so off he went. Shame!

Verdict: **TRUTH**

Leeds United pinched their white kit from Real Madrid

Some things in football you don't question: Manchester United play in red, Chelsea play in blue, and Leeds United, once one of the strongest teams in Europe, wear white. But has that always been the case?

★ And the truth is...

Leeds United were formed in 1919, and for the next 40 years wore a dark blue and gold kit. That is, until 1961, when manager Don Revie took over and insisted that the club play their home games in all white, like the all-conquering Real Madrid side of the time. A superstitious man, Revie believed that the switch to the kits sported by great players like Ferenc Puskás and Alfredo Di Stéfano would give his players confidence and self-belief. Leeds player at the time of the switch, Jack Charlton, later claimed it was so the players could see each other more easily!

Verdict: **TRUTH**

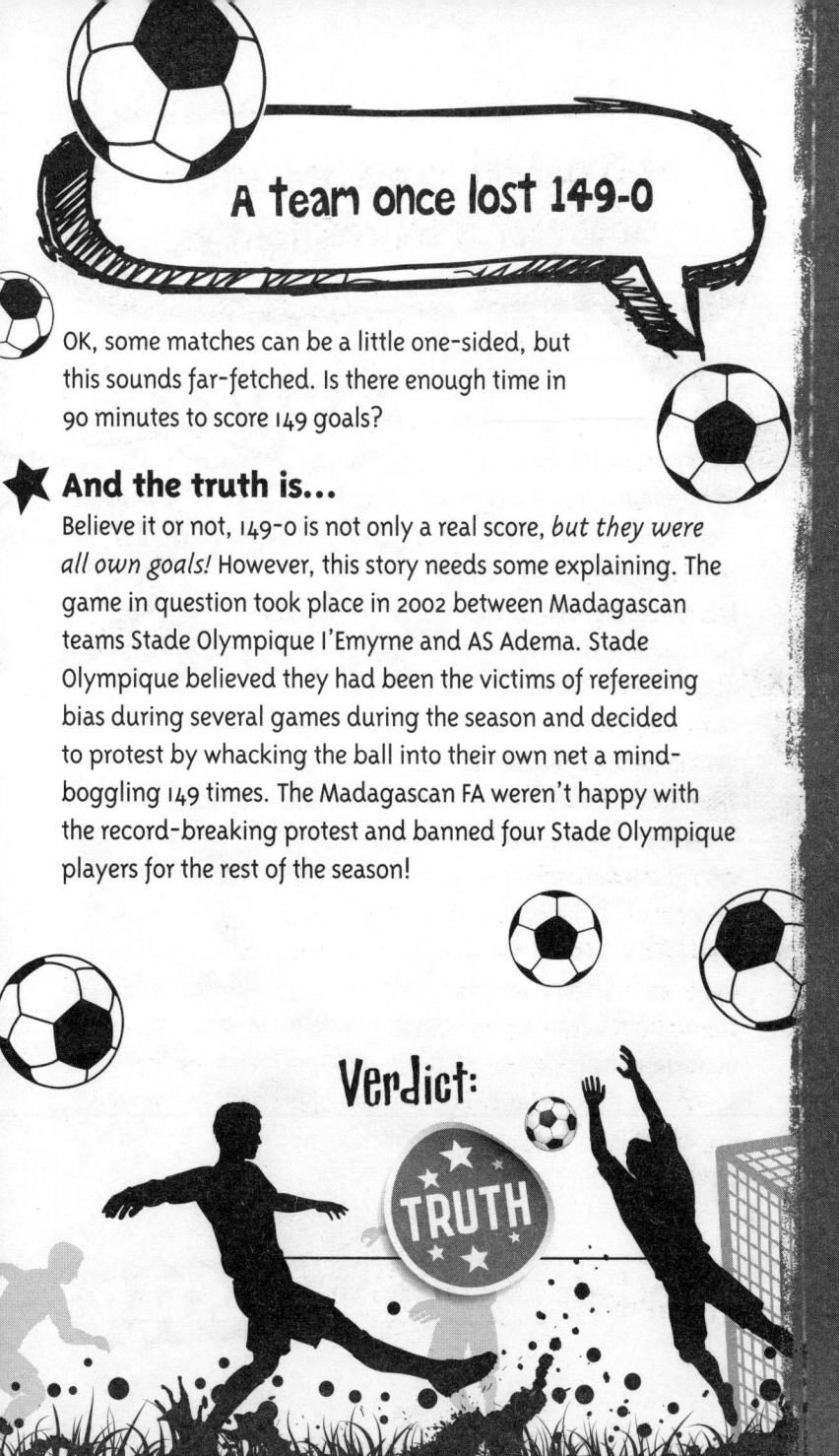

A team once lost 149-0

OK, some matches can be a little one-sided, but this sounds far-fetched. Is there enough time in 90 minutes to score 149 goals?

⭐ And the truth is...

Believe it or not, 149-0 is not only a real score, *but they were all own goals!* However, this story needs some explaining. The game in question took place in 2002 between Madagascan teams Stade Olympique l'Emyrne and AS Adema. Stade Olympique believed they had been the victims of refereeing bias during several games during the season and decided to protest by whacking the ball into their own net a mind-boggling 149 times. The Madagascan FA weren't happy with the record-breaking protest and banned four Stade Olympique players for the rest of the season!

Verdict:

TRUTH

Nottingham Forest are a team of Italian freedom fighters

No one disputes that Nottingham Forest have had a colourful history. For one, they were formed by a group of 'shinty' players (a type of hockey played in Scotland) who met in a room above a pub. Secondly, they were managed by Britain's most colourful and outspoken character, Brian Clough, who led the team to successive European Cups (the previous name for the Champions League) in 1979 and 1980. But Italian revolutionaries sounds a step too far.

★ And the truth is...

OK, it's far fetched, but there is some truth in it. Forest actually adopted their famous red tops in tribute to Italian general and politician Giuseppe Garibaldi, whose supporters were known as the 'red shirts'. Garibaldi's support of the rights of workers inspired a lot of support in the UK — so much so we named a biscuit after him!

Verdict: (we'd like it to be true, but actually)

A player's shirt number was once shown the red card

We've heard of players being red carded for removing their shirt, but we've never heard of the shirt itself getting a card. Sounds impossible?

 And the truth is...

Trust us, in football anything is possible! In 2002 Aberdeen's Moroccan striker Hicham Zerouaki was allowed to wear the number '0' on his back, after being nicknamed 'Zero' by Aberdeen fans. For the full season, he happily sported the unusual number on his back. However, the following season, Scottish League officials, the SPL, outlawed the number and Zerouaki had to go back to a normal, boring number like the rest of team.

ZEROUAKI

0

Verdict: (sort of true but mostly)

Teams can win a game on the amount of corners they take

Sure, the amount of corners a team gets during a match is a good indication of who is doing the most attacking, but they have no real value. Or do they?

⭐ And the truth is...

Well, believe it or not, before the penalty shoot-out was introduced, FIFA gave a lot of thought to using a corner count (how many corners each team had won during a game) as a way to decide drawn cup games. In fact, the method was even tried out live during the 1965 All-African Games tournament, when Congo beat Mali 7-2 on corners after the game ended 0-0. To be honest, though, we've never heard anything so daft, so we're not surprised it didn't catch on.

Verdict: [It used to be true, but now it's]

FOOTBALL RECORD BREAKERS

No 13: The world's worst penalty taker

Martin Palermo

Argentinian striker Palermo missed a record three penalties in a Copa America match against Colombia in 1999. His first penalty hit the bar and rebounded to safety, his second went over the top and then, incredibly, when he insisted on taking his country's third spot kick of the game the goalkeeper saved it! Full marks for determination. No marks for accuracy.

Where can I find myths about...

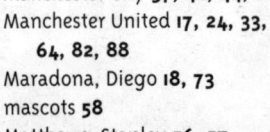

100%
SUCKER-PROOF

GUARANTEED!

Take a look at our other marvellously mythbusting titles...

Tip:
Turn over!

How NOT to be a sucker...